Read for a Better World™

T. REX

A First Look

TOM JACKSON

Lerner Publications ◆ Minneapolis

Educator Toolbox

Reading books is a great way for kids to express what they're interested in. Before reading this title, ask the reader these questions:

What do you think this book is about? Look at the cover for clues.

What do you already know about this dinosaur?

What do you want to learn about this dinosaur?

Let's Read Together

Encourage the reader to use the pictures to understand the text.

Point out when the reader successfully sounds out a word.

Praise the reader for recognizing sight words such as *has* and *was*.

TABLE OF CONTENTS

T. Rex

T. rex is a kind
of dinosaur.
The name is short for
Tyrannosaurus rex.

Tyrannosaurus rex
tuh-RA-nuh-saw-ruhs REKS

T. rex lived sixty-six
million years ago.
It was a hunter.

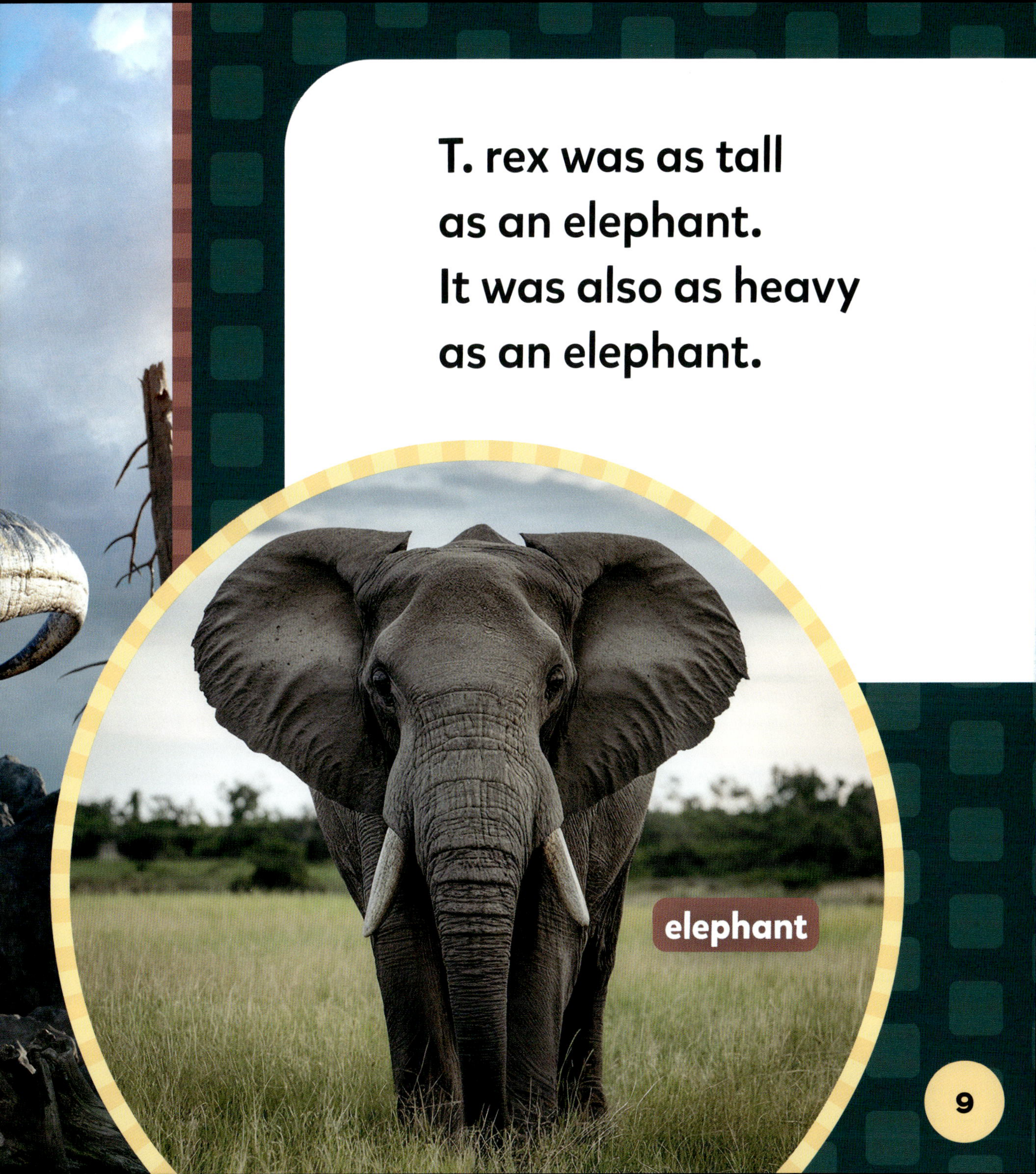

T. rex was as tall as an elephant. It was also as heavy as an elephant.

It walked on two legs.

How many legs do you have?

T. rex had a long tail.

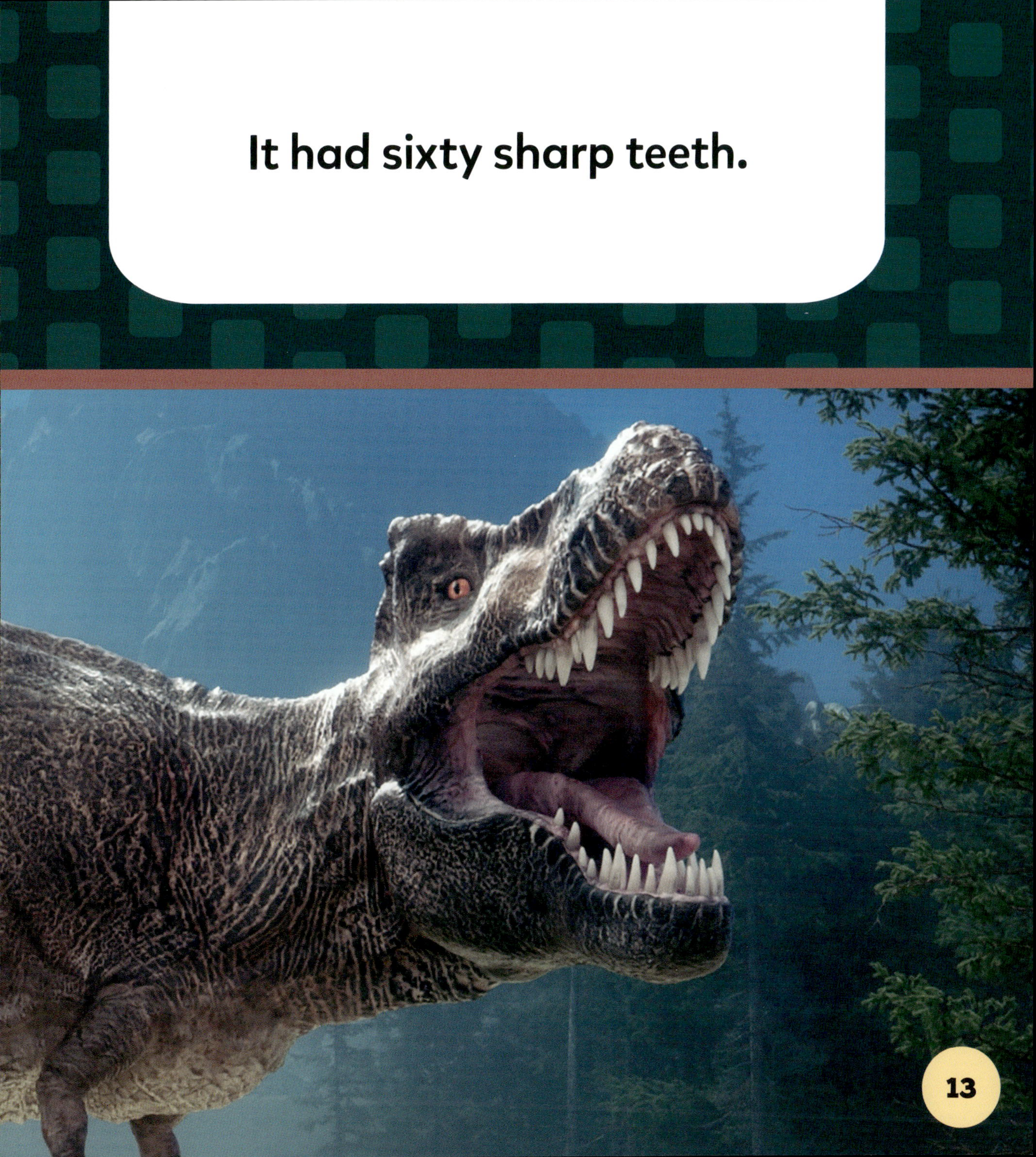

It had sixty sharp teeth.

teeth
tail
arm
leg

T. rex had big eyes.
It could see far away.

How would seeing well
help the dinosaur?

The dinosaur ate other animals. It had a strong bite.

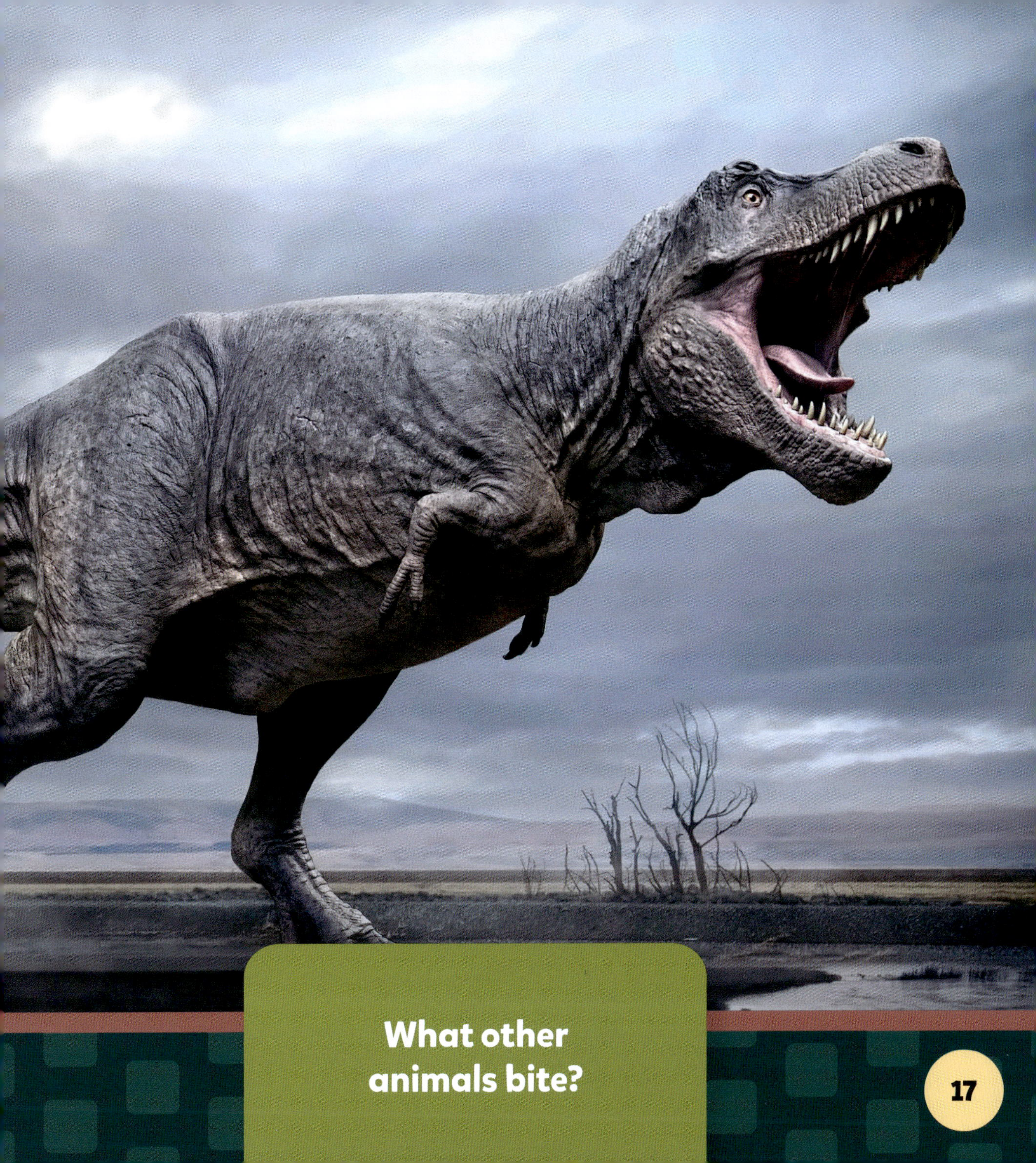

What other animals bite?

27

T. rex is not alive today. But people find its bones.

The bones teach us about how this dinosaur lived.

You Connect!

What is something you like about this dinosaur?

What else is as big as this dinosaur?

What other dinosaurs do you know about?

STEM Snapshot

Encourage students to think and ask questions like scientists. Ask the reader:

What is something you learned about this dinosaur?

What is something you noticed in the pictures of the dinosaur?

What is something you still don't know about this dinosaur?

Photo Glossary

Learn More

Beatty, Shannon and Gupta, Kritika. *My Encyclopedia of Very Important Dinosaurs.* New York: DK, 2024.

Dittmer, Lori. *Tyrannosaurus Rex*. Mankato, MN: Creative Education/Creative Paperbacks, 2024.

Vonder Brink, Tracy. *The Tyrannosaurus Rex.* New York: Crabtree Publishing, 2024.

Index

Photo Acknowledgments

The images in this book are used with the permission of: © Mark Turner/Dreamstime.com, p. 4; © Warpaint/Shutterstock Images, pp. 6–7, 8, 14; © RundumGuy/Shutterstock Images, pp. 9, 23 (elephant); © Orlando Florin Rosu/Dreamstime.com, pp. 10–11; © Matis75/Shutterstock Images, p. 12; © Orla/Shutterstock Images, pp. 13, 23 (teeth); © Elina/Shutterstock Images, pp. 15, 23 (eye); © PeartVision/ Shutterstock Images, pp. 16–17; © Nick Fox/Shutterstock Images, p. 18; © Toni Ponchai/Shutterstock Images, pp. 20, 23 (bones).

Cover Photograph: © Orlando Florin Rosu/Dreamstime.com

Design Elements: © Mighty Media, Inc.

Lerner Publications Company
An imprint of Lerner Publishing Group, Inc.
241 First Avenue North
Minneapolis, MN 55401 USA

For reading levels and more information, look up this title at www.lernerbooks.com.

Main body text set in Mikado a Medium. Typeface provided by Hannes von Doehren.

Library of Congress Cataloging-in-Publication Data

Names: Jackson, Tom, 1972-author
Title: T. rex : a first look / Tom Jackson.
Description: Minneapolis : Lerner Publications, [2026] | Series: Read about dinosaurs (read for a better world) | Includes bibliographical references and index. | Audience: Ages 5–8 | Audience: Grades K–1 | Summary: “How are a T. Rex and an elephant similar? Readers will find out in this nonfiction text with photorealistic images that help bring this prehistoric beast to life”—Provided by publisher.
Identifiers: LCCN 2025011282 (print) | LCCN 2025011283 (ebook) | ISBN 9798765689776 library binding | ISBN 9798348029036 paperback | ISBN 9798765697542 epub
Subjects: LCSH: Tyrannosaurus rex—Juvenile literature | Dinosaurs—Juvenile literature
Classification: LCC QE862.S3 J331 2026 (print) | LCC QE862.S3 (ebook) | DDC 567.912/9–dc23/eng/20250517

LC record available at https://lccn.loc.gov/2025011282
LC ebook record available at https://lccn.loc.gov/2025011283

Manufactured in the United States of America
1 - CG - 12/15/25